THE THOUGHTS OF
GOD

(The Rest Are Details)

**RESPONSE
TO
ALBERT EINSTEIN'S QUANDARY**

Stanisław Kapuściński

PUBLISHED BY INHOUSEPRESS

With profound thanks to

Albert Einstein

Without whom none of my conclusions
would have been possible.

This is my continued
Search for Secular Ethics

CONTENTS

1
HOW TO PEEK INTO
THE FUTURE

Strangely enough, to understand today, we must look deeply, and humbly, into the future. After all, we create our future today. Our future is the consequence of the thoughts we generate today. We create energies that dissipate and thus slow down their vibrations, creating our reality.

Also, beyond the Phenomenal Universe, there is no time. There is only the eternal present. This is where Einstein wanted to look to sate his insatiable curiosity, yet, being a scientist, he was obliged to look into the past.

This is the problem all scientists have to face. Science, many of them forget, is a method, not an accumulation of facts. Yet they base their observations on what is no more. Our world, our reality is in constant metamorphosis. That's what life is all about. Whatever is, will no longer be seconds from now.

In Universal terms, we are still a very primitive species. Our knowledge can only be guided by the awareness of systemic cycles that appear to spiral in the Universe in which we conduct our becoming. We know these cycles as the Ages of Zodiac. They give us an idea of how the Phenomenal reality works, or as

Einstein put it, what are: "The Thoughts of God".

In fact, Albert Einstein put it even more precisely: "*I want to know God's thoughts, the rest are details*"? he'd said. And... he very nearly did.

We can observe the consequences of these thoughts by observing the past. The Universe still exists, and therefore, whatever happened must have happened correctly, i.e. according to Universal Laws. The Laws must have been fulfilled, or we wouldn't be here anymore.

There would be no Universe. No matter how fluid.

I am referring, of course, to the Phenomenal Universe. The Universe we perceive with our most inadequate senses. There are countless aspects of reality we do not see, cannot touch, smell or be aware of. I am referring to all energies that vibrate at a rate faster than light; probably a countless number of them.

Nevertheless, we can attempt to understand the present by the same method. By projecting the evolutionary pattern of the past, we can attempt to imagine how it effects our present, or the mode of our becoming.

Finally, we can attempt to see our future by projecting the same thoughts, or patterns, into the future.

The present reality is the consequence of our past. By 'our' I am not referring to you and me, but to the infinity of thoughts generated by infinity of brains in the infinity of existence. And before that, by the cumulative effect of the trial and error generated by the Omnipresent Creative Energy, which, over infinity of becoming, manifested Omnipresent Consciousness.

And yet, we, you and I, contribute to our future.

To be more precise, we create our perception of the future. After all, in a reality that is in constant metamorphosis, reality we perceive is only an illusion. Our Being is the motivating energy within us. We, again, you and I, are in a perpetual state of Becoming.

The mega seasons of the Zodiac, which impose order over the mode of our Becoming, as with our annual cycles, vary in their purpose and results. While spring, summer, autumn, and winter, are all necessary to maintain a semblance of permanency over our perception of reality, each season fulfills a different function. The same is true of the Ages of the Zodiac, though its cycles deal with evolution of various species, rather than of individuals.

Please note.

Not of individuals but of the whole species.

The evolution of individuals is left to us: to the artificial intelligence generated by our brains. Our AI no only keeps us temporarily alive, but adds diversity to the reality in which we enjoy our Becoming.

To perceive the method of the Zodiac, we needn't go too far back. With each Age covering some 2160 years, theoretically, there ought to have been enough time to learn the lesson assigned to that period. And here we experience a profound problem.

Evolution of species is said to proceed at a pace somewhere between dead slow and dead slow. That is why the energies, which constitute our Becoming, are indestructible. They can, and do, constantly metamorphose their rate of vibrations, but they cannot be destroyed. In that sense, they have evolved to be immortal.

Yet, the cycles are not long enough, or our abilities are not sufficiently evolved, to absorb the lessons that are intended to be imprinted on our psyche. Hence, the Cycles of the Zodiac, and Becoming itself, is an eternal process. It is a process rather than a destination. In fact, only movement, hence change, is a sign of life. All that is static is the past. It is what the scientists study to learn what is. Regrettably, they only learn what was.

To repeat, the Phenomenal world, the reality we experience with our senses, is in a constant state of metamorphosis. The rates of vibrations of the energy, which make up our reality, are in constant flux.

~~~~~~~~

2
CREATIVE POWERS

The powers which humanity has inherited from the creative energy of the Omnipresent Consciousness are, obviously, not new. They have manifested in our species over thousands, probably millions, of years. Moses made use of them to liberate his people from Egyptian slavery. Since, various prophets made use of them.

There was a variety of 'miracles' performed by many people. One that fascinates me most, as it denies the presently known laws of physics, is bilocation, the 'miracle' of being in more than one place at the same time.

In addition to performing many other 'miracles', Padre Pio, also known as the Saint Pio of Pietrelcina, excelled in this ability.

Science has only just began to catch up with the possibility of this happening to atoms. And yet the concept of bilocation has appeared in early Greek philosophy, in Jewish and Christian mysticism, in Shamanism, Hinduism, and more recent philosophies such as Theosophy and New Age.

It is only a question of time before science will catch up with the powers welling within us. Regrettably, more often than not, a lot of time... It is generally accepted that evolution proceeds at a snail's pace.

Nevertheless, to my knowledge, such and other inherent powers reached their peak of manifestation in Yeshûa, the man later known as Jesus, who wielded quite unprecedented ability of metamorphosing energy by his indomitable will. He stated, quite unabashedly, that he (his ego) and his father (his Self) are one. He also suggested that the same could be said of all of us. After all, the prophets assured us that we are gods.

In other words, Yeshûa affirmed, on many occasions, that such powers are dormant within every one of us. Alas, the vast majority of people didn't listen. Still don't. Instead, they elevated Yeshûa to the status of God, and refused to listen to his teaching. Likewise, the previous statements by Hebrew prophets proclaiming that we are gods, fell on deaf ears.

People refused to be gods.

Still do.

They also refuse to believe that heaven is a state of Consciousness present, here and now, rather than a physical place to which they might retire to spend eternity in abject boredom. "Rest in Peace", is the damming statement, sentencing people to such abysmal condition.

~~~~~~~~

3
METAMORPHOSIS OF REALITY

This process became intellectually acceptable only since Albert Einstein had proven two fundamental Universal Laws. The first is that **"All is energy"**, and the second, that **"All (i.e. reality) is illusion"**. Needless to say, he was referring to the Phenomenal Reality.

Hence, to perform what is universally acceptable as miracles, in other words, to seemingly alter the physical shape or condition of matter, we no longer have to change material reality. All we need do it to manipulate the rate of vibrations of energies that create our reality.

Until Einstein's discovery, people accepted miracles at exclusively emotional level. This in no way diminished their authenticity, but it is very difficult for a human being steeped in a 'material' world to accept that no prophet, not even Yeshûa, could do it. Now we know that they substituted one illusion for another.

Why can't we all do that?

Because most of us still recognize our world, our reality, as made up of matter, and whatever we believe becomes our reality. Belief is the creative energy. The fact that atoms, of which virtually all 'things' are made, are 99.9999999999996% empty space is hard to accept. That is why Einstein admitted that the illusion of solid world is a *very persistent illusion.*

Today, atoms are in fact recognized as points in space with "non-zero" mass. The mass is too small for our ability to measure it. We lack words to describe it. Hence, they are just... points in space.

~~~~~~~~

4
DIVERSITY AND BALANCE

While there is probably an infinite number of Universal Laws, there are two Laws that have a direct effect on our everyday life. The first is the **Law of Diversity**, and the second is the **Law of Balance**.

They seem quite straightforward.

To implement both the evolutionary process evolved cyclic progression. While climatic seasons control the individual becoming, the Zodiac controls the evolution of the species. While evolution requires diversity, balance controls the integrity of Oneness.

Some microorganisms are derived from a single cell, display a single DNA, and thus are identical. Yet bacteria, in their struggle for survival can act in radically different ways. While parthenogenesis (reproduction of an ovum without fertilization) still exists in some invertebrates and lower plants, splitting of sexual organs vastly increases the diversity of a species. As the complexity of any organism increases, so do its chances of survival.

More complex organisms, have given up hermaphroditic abilities, to increase diversity, and thus the chances of survival of a species.

The more evolved is any species the more it contributes to the diversity of the Phenomenal Universe. Human species has reached uniqueness in this field.

So much for the survival of the individuals.

Those same individuals, perhaps due to their individuality are capable to react differently to both, the same as well of to different stimuli. Since, as we already know, all is energy, different reactions set up different rates of vibrations of energy. Those diverse rates of vibrations of energy are responsible for the continuous expansion of the Phenomenal Universe.

This is an eternal process.

~~~~~~~~

5
AGE OF AQUARIUS

Even as children, when coming of age, leave home, losing the protection of their parents, so in this new Age, the Age of Aquarius, humanity is intended to come of age. Our loss is that of kings, queens, presidents, prime ministers, as well as presumed leaders and their appointed emissaries of various 'intellectual' and/or religious groups. The illustrious places of learning will lose their luster. The experts in various fields will lose their authority, as most people will begin to rely on their own research, relying on diverse sources. Diverse knowledge will gain greater following than narrow expertise.

It has been said that, ultimately, a true expert knows almost everything about almost nothing. The opposite of this sentiment will become more desirable.

The same will apply to leaders in all fields, not the least of which will be various religions. People will strive to develop their own philosophies, rather than follow the precepts imposed by others. The maxim that knowledge lies within you will gain new ground.

The consequence of this trend will lead to enormous increase in diversity of thought, hence of the Universe.

Most of us appear to be unaware that societal

stratification pervades all fauna. There are level of leadership established among virtually all species.

Unbeknownst to religious fraternities there is no "mega-brain" of an overseeing deity controlling evolution. The Omnipresent Consciousness is infinite in ALL potentialities. Good or evil are characteristics of the Phenomenal reality, not of the Infinite Potential. Hence, evolution proceeds by trial and error.

This is how evolution works.

The seed (idea) is born in the in the Infinite Potential, the AI convert it into the energy of thought. It fulminates, and a few of us pick it up at conscious level, while others don't bother to search for it. I find it amazing that some 2000 years ago the evangelists who wrote the Bible had already known this. They seem to have been more advanced in metaphysical knowledge than we are today.

In Matthew 13, the process is described as follows:

"The kingdom of heaven is like a mustard seed, which a man took and planted in his field. Though it is the smallest of all your seeds, yet when it grows, it is the largest of garden plants and becomes a tree, so that the birds of the air come and perch in its branches."

Kingdom of Heaven is, of course, the state of Consciousness that is guided by Self, not by ego. When the two combine, the ego becomes immortal.

Humanity always consisted of the Few, the Many, and, regrettably, what I call the Third Party. The Few, very few, heard the silent voice, and followed it. The

Many heard it, but didn't have the perseverance to follow its dictates. The members of Third Party were too busy with the illusion of the Phenomenal reality to even listen to the silent voice within.

Regrettably, only the Few advance.

Most tread water, or even devolve to a lower stage of consciousness. Individualization of the Omnipresent Consciousness is not to set us apart, only to add diversity to the Phenomenal Universe. The spark of immortality is identical in every one of us. What differs is our awareness of our Source. The sum-total of the accumulated experience generated by our artificial intelligence is our soul. Our ego is no more than the product of our artificial intelligence generated by our brain. In a way, we are no more than a transient reflection of the potential within us. Until, in the fullness of time, our ego and our Higher Self become ONE.

Once we accept that the Bible has NOTHING to do with any religion, but that it is a magnificent compendium of knowledge gathered over thousands of years, we should discover many answers to today's questions. Only, please, don't tell any preachers about it. They'll twist it beyond recognition. Once we externalize the 'divine' energy of the Creative Potential, we regress to pre-Edenic mentality, but without being aware of it. We shall revert to a purely reactive mode of Becoming.

The first step in the new Age of Aquarius is: *"do your own research"*.

Don't believe experts who make a living, probably much better than yours, for your money.

Don't ignore them, but check them. There are some excellent people among them, but they, too, are only the Few. Then, there are a few more from among the Many that are trying, but not making it.

Not quite, but at least they are trying.

The rest of the learned PhDs are as pathetically inept and the majority in any group. Yes, *any* group. The three groups refer to their state of Consciousness, not to their social, educational or financial standing.

The Age of Aquarius will slowly eliminate educational and financial differentials. Don't be fooled by the powerful trying desperately to hold onto their 'worldly' power. Their world is disappearing. Within the next 2000 years, only the inner powers will prevail.

During the Age of Aquarius humanity will rebel against being told what and how to conduct their lives. For the first time since we fought for survival in the wilds of nature, we shall, once again be forced to stand on our own feet.

Only now, to stand on our 'spiritual' feet.

The great conglomerates, the industrial, commercial, and political powerhouses, will begin to shudder at the onset of the new rates of vibration of energy. The 'masses' will rebel against them unaware that, until recently, those very organizations provided the bread and butter of their physical survival. New vibrations, new energies, will flood the artificial consciousness generated by the (biologically superb) phenomenal brains of the masses. They will begin to suspect that there is more to life than material wellbeing.

Yet, most of all, for the first time in thousands of years, people, humanity at large, will stop relying on an imagined divinity they called God, to look after them, particularly in their hours of need.

For the last 2000 years, billions of Christians, and almost as many Moslem, ignored the teaching of Yeshûa, whom they ordained as their great prophet, if not God. Yes, even the Moslem refer to the Bible as a revelation.

> *The Quran mentions the Torah, the Zabur ("Psalms") and the Injil ("Gospel") as being revealed by God to the prophets Moses, David and Jesus respectively in the same way the Quran was revealed to Muhammad.*
>   (Wikipedia)

It appears that most Muslim, the followers of Islam, don't know about it. Pity. And, according to Yeshûa (Jesus) told them that "Heaven is within you", and that "my father (God), is in heaven". Whereas according to Muslim there are seven Heavens. Hence, their One God must have a split personality, if He resides in each one of them. Or some of their heavens don't have His presence.

I prefer Yeshûa's version.

However, whichever version we adopt, nothing helped.

Saints, modern day prophets, were equally ignored.

People continued to ignore biblical teaching and looked up to the clouds for their salvation.

2000 years of ignorance, fuelled by religions hungry for power to control peoples' minds, have passed. And now? Yes, religions, too, will fall.

People will begin to search for great abilities within their own inner selves, within our own minds, their Consciousness. They will search for their own inherent potential. They will no longer expect others to feed their bodies, but will search for the food to feed their minds, their inherent abilities.

Slowly they will discover the Infinite Potential ever-present within them. Ever-present within us. The ancient statement "Ye are gods" will take on a new meaning.

It will not be easy.

It will take time.

Around... 2160 years...

Yet, even as we, as individuals, all go through childhood, teen years, adulthood, and old age, so too the whole human species rotates in cycles of some 26,000 years.

However, to accomplish all that is intended by each Age of the Zodiac, to make it come about, we must make sure that we do not put "new wine into old skins". We must abandon the past to make room, in our minds, in our awareness, for the new.

~~~~~~~

6
PLUTO EFFECT

Although they maybe completely unaware of this, the challenge for present leaders of the world, of the present state of the constantly metamorphosing reality, is to completely destroy the authority with which they have been entrusted. Their job is to free people from looking for help from the so-called authorities.

This is called the Pluto Effect.

Originally, in Greek mythology, Pluto ruled the Underworld, they knew as Hades. He was also known as "the Wealthy One", or "the Giver of Wealth", which may account for the followers of religions sinking into the consciousness of abject materiality, let alone greed.

Later, according to various Christian denominations, Hades became known as "the place of departed spirits". Later still, when the "carrot and the stick" philosophy took over from the concept of Christian love, Hades became also known as Hell, and Pluto the God of Death. The leaders of Christianity spared no effort to scare their believers into absolute obedience.

Since, Pluto, until recently a planet, has been recognized as a transforming energy. It symbolizes the subconscious forces. It is also associated with renewal and rebirth. It represents endings and new beginnings, as well as spiritual growth and rebirth.

The function of the **Pluto Effect**, and of all people whose function is to carry out its dictates, is to make sure that the masses of people (the Third Party) start thinking for themselves.

However, unless we have learned the lesson of the Age of Pisces, we are in grave danger of destructive anarchy.

The Age of Pisces had been intended to show us the irrepressible oneness of the human species. This was an expression of the centripetal force that manifested itself as the energy of love.

If we haven't learned this singular trait during the last 2160 years, then Pluto Effect might fill the void of the absence of leadership with destructive anarchy. Unless we have learned to love one another, a different species might take over the Earth.

It is that simple.

We must never forget that we are not our bodies, nor even our minds, but we are *Individualizations of the Energy of the Omnipresent Consciousness*. The real 'we' cannot die. I AM is immortal.

But, if we fail in our purpose, our AI, our artificial intelligence, can, and will, be recycled. Unbeknownst to our astrophysicists, that is what the Black Holes are for. They accelerate the rates of vibrations of energies to their original condition. To the rate of vibration of the Omnipresent Creative Energy of which all "things" are made.

Yet, we mustn't expect immediate results. The dictum that 'Many' are called but 'Few' are chosen remains in force. It is a peripheral aspect of the Universal Laws dealing with the evolution of various species. And over the next 2000 years, the self-reliance of an individual will constitute the next gigantic step in the evolution of the human species. Perhaps all the others, too?

It will be up to us.

After all, the whole purpose of evolution is to produce a state of consciousness that manifests the essence of the expression:

YE ARE GODS

There is no other purpose to the evolution. Yet, only a Few will make the grade. The rest will be recycled to try again, and again. *Ad infinitum.*

We must never forget that we are vortices of Energy. What is more difficult to accept is that the energy at the highest, in fact infinite, rate of vibration is manifested within us as our higher Self. This infinite rate being both, omnipresent and individualized makes it hard to perceive with our limited senses. Yet, it is within us, even as everywhere. The quantum field attests to that.

We advance by enriching the Phenomenal reality; by enhancing its diversity. We are the instruments of the Omnipresent Energy of Creative Consciousness.

The Pluto Effect reminds us of this truth.

The fundamental difference, which we shall experience from the previous age, will be that the *Few* will no long order, or command, the *Many* to act in any particular way. Instead, they'll serve as an example. Let us never forget, that the *Few* are defined by the power they wield, not by any human definition of good or evil. And power is defined by the ability to manipulate the rates of vibrations of various energies. We, in our ignorance, refer to such power as miracles. In fact, this same power rests within every one of us. Only... we need faith to reawaken it, and then humility to submit to it.

We must sublimate our egos to a higher authority.

This is difficult for a number of reasons.

The first reason is that we need our egos to survive in the phenomenal reality. On the other hand, according to our Self (*i.e.:* the higher authority), we must place the good of the species above that of our own. The instinct of self-preservation is the culprit in this transfer of allegiance. What we find difficult to accept is that we are NOT our bodies, nor even our brains, but we are intended to use both to enrich the phenomenal reality.

The strange thing is that the truly great men always knew this. They willingly offered their lives for the good of others. We pinned medals to their chests, built statues in their honour, or even elevated them to the status of sainthood. Yet, the 'masses' would never dream of following in their footsteps.

No matter how unsuccessfully, they preferred to serve to god of mammon, the god of covetousness, of perennial greed. The Pluto Effect will attempt to remedy this malady.

As for the new 'leaders', they will show rather than talk about the human potential. They will lead by example, not by the carrot and the stick methodology. They will dangle tasty pieces of metaphysical tidbits in front of people's noses until we, the masses, develop a hunger to create and taste this divine ambrosia on our own.

Yet, even though not all of us will succeed, many will do so in vastly greater numbers than in the previous Age. Perhaps they'll sense that for another such chance, for the repeat of the Age of Aquarius, they'll have to wait a while. The Great Age of the Zodiac takes some 26,000 years. This knowledge might induce them to try harder.

There is one other item of vital importance. During the initial stage, under the influence of the *Pluto Effect*, the Third Party, which, due to its relative ignorance is easiest to control by the Energy of the Omnipresent Consciousness, will elect leaders who will aid the changeover of the social, political, and religious systems. They may seem, and in fact be, of destructive nature, but what they are in fact destroying is the abortive system than no longer serves humanity.

Empires will fall. As will the emperors.

From the transient anarchistic patterns, systems will emerge that will serve humanity as a whole, rather than individual people. Gradually people will become aware of the inherent oneness of us all.

A little, like a global family.

What few of us appear to realize is the fact, mentioned above, that in spite of the presumption of free will, we are all instruments of the Omnipresent Consciousness, that advances us, as a species, on the path, which, over thousands of years, will advance us towards our individual realizations.

As I'm sure you noticed, the overwhelming

majority of us have a very, very long way to go.

Furthermore, one of the principle intents of the Pluto Effect is to reduce the absurdly burgeoning human population, often at the expense of most other species. Though it may sound absurd and even heartless, the two World Wars helped, but they were not enough. The virus, known as COVID-19, is instrumental in doing so at present, (as had been other plagues in the past), but it cannot be successful without our cooperation. Two factors might advance it towards relative success, sadly: *stupidity and greed.*

Stupidity, in addition to ignorance, confers the reliance on ego, and greed is the consilient component of our persistent illusion of the phenomenal reality. Greed and ego both serve the survival of an individual, and not of the species. The present pandemic offers us ample examples of both in today's reality. The behaviour of the masses is a vivid example of both. Having been told to wear masks and maintain a reasonable distance from each other, they, those masses, reject being told what to do.

Their egos object.

They rebel, in vast crowds, against any suggestion that, they construe, as limiting their freedom. The vast global overpopulation forces people to be fairly close to each other, a little like rats in a global cage, affecting the behaviour of the masses in ever-increasing numbers. Also, fear of the unknown fuels their dispositions.

And their numbers are great.

Since the beginning of the Industrial Revolution in seventeen hundreds (the year 1700), when the world population was around 610 million, we managed to increase this number to 7,794,798,739 people, or nearly 7.8 billion. Is there any wonder that nature guided by the Universal Laws, began to take steps to curtail our sexual tendencies?

To date, no measures sufficed.

Overwhelming droughts leading to extensive fires of thousands of acres of forests didn't help. Nor did the increase in the number of tropical storms and hurricanes, monsoons, floods and suchlike, all, most probably caused by the rise in the global temperature, referred to as global warming. We continued to pollute our air thus increasing carbon dioxide in the air.

Nature seems helpless.

Since the pandemic coronavirus was recognized some nine months ago, in South Asia alone 29 million birth were expected, compared to 200 thousand worldwide death, purportedly due to COVID-19. The virus didn't help. We are still spreading like vermin. Will anything stop us?

Or shall we, eventually, starve to death.

We can expect more global changes, such as shifting of magnetic poles. They are moving already. They might play havoc with world communications, on the reliance on GPSs, and therefore air travel.

The list goes on.

Yet, if such measures will not work, nature might turn to a different tack. As mentioned above, it produced a virus. All we needed to defend from it was to wear a mask, and keep a few feet distance from other members of our species.

No such luck. Egocentricity rose to new heights. As mentioned above, the masses refused to submit to any regulations that impede, in any way, their freedom of action or behaviour. No matter how dangerous to themselves and others. No matter how selfish.

I'd suggest that volcanic eruptions and earthquakes might be next. Then we can expect extensive global inundations, caused by the rise in sea levels, due to the melting of all icebergs. Plus mass starvation, and unnecessary suffering. Unnecessary because, after all, unbeknownst to most us, we create our reality. Not just as individuals, but also as a species. Even a mentally limited species such as we are.

Yet even this might have been overcome by the dexterity of the human ingenuity, if it weren't for the overwhelming, frankly absurd greed of the so-called "upper classes". I'll share with you just one example from my own country.

The Canadian government, in their wisdom, in response to the pandemic, proposed that the middle seat on Air Canada airplanes be left empty, to provide at least a marginal separation between the passengers. A lot less than the physical distancing of 6 feet advocated elsewhere, but, surely, better than nothing.

It worked for a little while.

Yet, soon, it stopped. Greed was the reason. The management refused to lose the money they'd get for the middle seat.

This might have been more acceptable if it weren't for the insatiable greed of the people at the helm.

In recent years, the average income of Canadians has risen to $51K per annum. It is a reasonable wage that offers all the comforts to people of reasonable tastes. At the same time, last year, the compensation of the Air Canada CEO and jumped by 28% to $11.5 million. Yes, also per annum.

Such greed should send their chief executive, to hell on a one-way trip, without a parachute. This man needs to be recycled.

However, not to take all the credit for such exorbitant manifestation of greed, let us note that in the USA, the average annual compensation of the CEO's of the 350 largest US firms was, in 2018, around $14 million (each!), up from $12.7 million in 2017.

So much can be said for democratic equality in the country of the free, the USA.

Nevertheless, just to cheer you up, these are relative peanuts compared to salary/winnings of Christiano Ronaldo, which, in 2017, was $58 million; Lionel Messi's, $53 million; and LeBron James's a measly, $31.2 million. And yet some of us can sink even lower. According to Forbes, as of March 18, 2020, there were 2,095 billionaires worldwide. On the other hand the United Nations Food and Agriculture Organization estimates that about **815 million people** of the 7.6 billion people in the world, or one in ten, were suffering from chronic undernourishment in 2016.

Bon appétit, billionaires.

Furthermore, while there are many millionaires

who are very generous, offering millions of dollars to charity, there are also the silent majority of them, who will forever remain nameless, and who are to a degree responsible for starvation of some inept levels of society. Many politicians adorn those ranks. The others are the televangelists.

Although they might be geniuses at making money, I'm not sure they are of the same species. I don't believe they belong in the human race.

Yet, there is one other aspect of the period that initially escaped my notice. Reading Internet news, and some comments on the TV, it is becoming apparent that the population of the US is sinking into an abysmal well of fear. They are not even sure what is it that they fear, but their behaviour makes it quite apparent. I wonder if they feel something, subliminally, that the rest of us do not, as yet, perceive.

As for making money, Carl Sagan once said: "Sheer genius is no cure against being dead wrong." This might well apply to all our merchants of greed.

~~~~~~~

7
FREE WILL

Do we, the people, under the guidance of our illustrious scientific, political or religious, leaders enjoy free will?

Very much so?

Or... only up to a point. If we abuse or misunderstand our leaders' 'benevolent' guidance we are incarcerated in a lunatic asylum, or jail, or, if a little later, we are sent to Hell.

There are a number of events our leaders forced us to partake in, all over the world. In the **WWI**, there had been some 20 million deaths plus 21 million wounded.

Yet, only a few years later, thanks again to our leaders, we followed their orders, by enlisting into the armed forces, and march, joyously, into **WWII.** There was an impressive progress in our devolution. In **World War II** the estimated total of death rose to 85 million, which was about 3% of the established world population of 2.3 billion at the time.

Should we be lead into another war, a **WW III**, with the present population of 7.8 billion, we could look forward to at least, 288 million death (yes, that's 288,000,000), and this without taking into account our improved killing technology.

With, at present, nine countries, (the US, UK, Russia, France, China, India, Pakistan, Israel, and North Korea,) being armed with nuclear weapons, we could look forward our destructive power in billions of lives.

Now that would be an unprecedented progress.

Backwards?

So much for our leadership and our free will.

Are you sure we are on the right 'evolutionary' track? Or are we devolving at an astonishing rate. As already stated in the chapter on EVOLUTION, we appear to evolve in cycles of some 26,000 years, apparently, each time starting from fresh. Each cycle starts at the very peak of the evolution reached in the previous cycle, and, slowly and often painfully, advances to the next level. This is not subject to our free will. This is the fundamental Universal Law

Enter the Age of Aquarius. By observing the early years, by its onset that manifests in the *Pluto Effect*, the sooner we give up our leadership let alone the concept of free will, the more lives we are likely to save.

Not that 7.8 billion is worth saving.

Unfortunately, human concept of free will does not discriminate between the Few, the Many, or the Third Party. Members at the bottom of *all* the three groups die with equal facility. Hence, the Universe instituted cycles of seasons to control our 'evolution'. Only the best is retained, the rest is recycled. That could be why the symbolic start in the Biblical Garden of Eden purports to have started with just one man, Adam. And even he was bereft of the subconscious, which Eve provided in due course. How many pre-humanoid entities preceded him we are unlikely to find out, but it doesn't bid well for our distant future. Let us hope that more than one of us makes the grade. If not, then, I suspect, a different species will take over the evolutionary process from us. After all, the dinosaurs lived in the Mesozoic Era, between 245 and 66 millions years ago. And they already evolved from socket-toothed archosaurs.

As we are all fully aware, there are not many archosaurs around. Not even their descendant, dinosaurs. Shall we follow in their footsteps? Are any or us worth preserving longer then they had been?

Was Adam really the only one around? Was he the only humanoid who reached out for the forbidden fruit of knowledge?

Or do the cycles go on, and on...
And so on... and so forth.
Eternally...?
Or will the semblance of our free will change the evolutionary currents...

We must never forget that our scientists already confirmed that the Phenomenal Universe is eternal. We used to think that it was 13.8 billion years old. Since then, Stephen Hawking and Thomas Hertog, both theoretical physicists, pushed the onset of our Universe into infinity.

Believers in various religions must be pleased. After all, if the Universe were only 13.8 billion years, what would their God have been doing before that time?

And to assure that we continue to evolve, our Universe will continue to expand. Also, forever after. That alone should keep God busy. On the other hand, Einstein assured us that our reality is all... just an illusion.

Albeit, *"a very persistent one"*.

As the indestructible energy of the Omnipresent Universal Consciousness has Its being outside time, space, or any other limitation, it is not subject to human temporal scale. As mentioned, the Ages can be divided into periods of about 2160 'human', or earthy years.

Fortunately (or not), even such long periods of time are only tiny fractions of eternity. During the age of Pisces we have been intended to learn to "love one another". We managed to fail miserably. The **WWII** is a convincing example. Even though, these Ages are but fractions of the Year of the Zodiac, which last for 26,000 years. Hence there is a bigger game in town.

Remember the dinosaurs?

Even so, without taking into account the concept of reincarnation, none of us would be able to take advantage of this Universal temporal generosity.

Thus, let us make it absolutely clear. Whether the dinosaurs do so or not:

We, the human species, do enjoy free will.
And we bear 100% consequences of our actions.

As for the Generosity of the Universe, as Albert Einstein has pointed out, all is illusion. What we killed in world wars were not the Individualizations of the Universal Creative Consciousness, only the illusory containers, which we use to learn the consequences of our actions.

Enter Karma.

Karma serves to restore balance.

The Universal Creative Energy loves diversity, which accounts for the ever-expanding Phenomenal Universe. This diversity is provided by the artificial intelligence generated by the brains of the units of Individualization such as we are. One of the best examples of our contribution to such diversity was Isaac Newton. Sir Isaac was a mathematician, physicist, astronomer, theologian and author. A diversity of interests equal, if not exceeding that, of Leonardo da Vinci. Sir Isaac described his own predilections as those of a "natural philosopher".

A truly great man.

He was the first to perceive and define one of the fundamental Laws of the Universe.

For every action, he said, *there is an equal and opposite reaction.*

This Law, alone, assures the balance necessary to sustain the existence of our Phenomenal Universe. Without it, we'd disperse into the infinity of space, or collapse into a pinpoint of a Black Hole.

We don't. Hence Sir Isaac was right.

Yet... his magnificent perception that came to us only a few centuries ago (Isaac Newton vacated his body in his sleep on March 31, 1726), did little more than reestablish the seemingly esoteric Law of Karma which mystics proclaimed for thousands of years. A little like Einstein's concept that:

"**Science** without **religion** is lame, **religion** without **science** is blind.

You decide.

~~~~~~~~

8
THE NEW AGE

There is a single lesson to learn for the Aquarians. Although this Age has been prophesied for thousands of years, (see my exegeses entitled ISAIAH 9:6 and the DECALOGUE) only now, this magnificent awareness of our potential will begin dawning on the masses. Yes, even on the Third Party. Many, of course, will reject it as yet another superstition, but many more than ever before will discover, within themselves, the silent voice which will begin to govern their lives.

People will begin to discover the incredible creative potential within them.

They will begin to discover their true Selves.

This will not be as surprising as we might imagine. Every potential within us has already, at some time or another, been demonstrated in the past. Jesus and countless mystics, a few saints and some gurus and fakirs have demonstrated, repeatedly, our abilities.

At the time, such abilities, being in complete denial of science of the day, have been and remained, *per force*, the domain of religion. In the Age of Aquarius they will emerge slowly from the realm of mysticism, and gradually will permeate and be accepted by the scientific fraternity.

Hence, they will become accessible to all who wish to study their secrets.

This magnificent awakening will completely change our attitude towards our civilization, our technology, even to methods of education. The direction or the orientation of learning will not be directed outwards, but inwards. The ancient prophecies will begin manifesting in the most unexpected places, among the most unexpected people. We shall discover that ALL power comes from within. Not from our phenomenal bodies, not from material possessions, not from any aspect of the illusory reality, but from the inexhaustible creative power ever-present as Creative Energy within us.

~~~~~~~~

9
THE NEW REALITY

We must never forget that, with the exception of the Few, the vast majority of humanity was, and still is, in a devolutionary mode. Every 26,000 years, or so, the evolutionary cycles are reversed. We return, once again, to what the religions have metaphorically called the Garden of Eden. We return to a reality in which we, Homo sapiens, are aware of our true nature. In which we have been, like the rest of nature, in a reactive mode. A mode in which, with the exception of the human species, the rest of the phenomenal reality, still is.

We revert to individualizations of our original intent.

We become aware of our true nature.

Yet, the creative impulse of the Omnipresent Consciousness will not be denied.

We begin as pure energy (individualized units of Consciousness), and gradually acquire "skins", i.e. phenomenal, seemingly material, forms. They are not real, but their rate of vibration of energy is sufficiently slowed down to give an impression of a solid substance.

We call them our bodies. And those, too are subject to irrepressible impulse of creative energy. Hence evolution of the phenomenal body had to reflect the evolutionary impulse within. It had to be an image of its Source. Of the Creative Energy.

The result was the evolution of a system that would be self-sustaining. This led to the evolution of the brain. Not just in the humans, but in all living matter.

The microorganisms such as bacteria, archaea, fungi, protozoa, algae, and viruses are under direct control of the Omnipresent Consciousness.

There are, however, genetically driven changes that occur in microorganisms. They, for instance bacteria, can evolve quickly, because they reproduce at a fast rate. This can lead to mutations, and the resulting new strains. In this way the Omnipresent Creative Consciousness retains control over higher life forms. Through rapid mutation, bacteria can become resistant to antibiotics, and other defensive measures produced by us. Our scientists refer to such resistance natural selection. I call it the overriding control of the Omnipresent Consciousness. It is only a question of semantics.

We must never forget that even the latest (2016) review of human microbiome, allows for an average human to be playing host to around 100 trillion microbes. I'd suggest their numbers speaks volumes about who, or what, influences control over our phenomenal bodies.

As for our evolution, perhaps we ought to note that number of genes in all of our microbiome is 200 times greater than in human genome. And that, bearing in mind, that each cell in a human body contains about 25,000 to 35,000 genes. And, by the way, a gene is an abbreviation of DNA, or deoxyribonucleic acid, that carries our hereditary material. Ours, appears to be 200 times smaller than that of the microbes residing within us.

Are you sure you want to be just your body?

Or would you rather be more than that.

And this brings us to our brain. It came later. Yet, way back when, Adam reached for the tree of knowledge and ate the apple, in preference of eating the fruit of the tree of life.

Again, this, like the rest of the Bible, is all symbolic. The 'apple' leads to the evolution of Ego, while the tree of life would have supported the Self. Ego, as we already know, is product of artificial intelligence generated by our brain. It tends to separate us from each other. Self brings us together again. You can read more on this subject in my brief exegesis SELF EGO VIRUS.

No matter...

I am fairly sure that, to this day, in spite of an average of 100 billion neurons in our heads, the vast majority of us are quite unaware of the microbiome that fulminates within us. And, most probably, controls many aspects of our life.

Indirectly, of course. After all, our microbiome is only a means. The real control is the Omnipresent Consciousness. The theoretical physicists are on the right track with their quantum field theory (QFT). They are already moving particles to fields. All they need do is to convert it all to energy, and they'll be home.

They'll advance from the kindergarten to the primary school. Well, they will be in the antechamber of the Omnipresent Consciousness. The knowledge is already within them, only ego stands in the way.

Thank Heavens we're immortal!

Originally, the concept of Eden had been intended to mean that some mammals have reached a vague awareness of their individuality, and began the slow process of reinforcing their individualization. This awareness led to their first contribution of the Universal diversity. Let us never forget that the Universe is replete with intelligent life forms that perform the task of adding to the phenomenal diversity for countless billions of years.

Perhaps... eternally?

A single look at the starry sky at night should be sufficient to convince every single doubting Thomas, that the phenomenal Universe is infinite. I read recently that some astronomers claim that we can 'observe' only two galaxies, the Milky Way and the Andromeda galaxy.

I am not an astronomer, yet this sounds to me like utter, unabashed, nonsense.

Great many of pinpoints of light in the night sky are not stars. They are galaxies, each holding some 100 billion stars. Those galaxies are so far away that they appear to us like stars. The Universe is infinite. Remember?

And so is our future, better described as the "Eternal Present." Time is a dimension of the phenomenal Universe only. We, you and I, and every other thinking entity, are more than the phenomenal enclosures in which we conduct our becoming. We are beings of pure, indestructible energy.

Returning to Eden... The unfortunate consequence of

"Adam's" action lead to increased desire of achieving, no matter how transient, result, rather than enhancement of the creative process itself. This, in turn, lead to the birth of the ego, or that, which defines our differences by our possessions, rather than our irrepressible unity.

As mentioned, the purpose of evolution is intended to add to the diversity or the Universe, ever remembering that the Phenomenal Universe consists exclusively of energy.

Energy that creates a transient illusion.

Hopefully Albert Einstein has proven this to everyone's satisfaction, in spite of the persistent illusory 'evidence' to the contrary.

Hence ideas contributed by individualized units of Consciousness, i.e. by ever entity capable of generating the *energy of thought*, contributes to the inevitable constant expansion of the phenomenal Universe.

Thoughts are 'things'.

Material things are an illusion.

This creative process is as eternal and omnipresent as the Energy of Creative Consciousness, which manifests at an infinite rate of vibration. To repeat, it exists beyond time or space. Infinity cannot be defined.

As the rates of vibrations slow down, they manifest in Phenomenal Universe as transient, illusory reality. Reality in which we, and all life, enjoy our becoming, is defined by constant change.

Nevertheless, the Potential Universe is, always was, and always will be omnipresent.

To conclude, we should never forget that the formula of "the Few, the Many, and the Third Party" applies to all levels of society, education and professions. It refers to the state of Consciousness, not to the inherited or acquired, often erroneous, knowledge or phenomenal possessions. Our schools and universities teach what was. What is for fragments of eternity is invariably an illusion. What it seldom teaches is what could be. Hence the so-called education is always *passée*. Only very few scientists who venture into the unknown advance our knowledge, the rest follow like sheep, as in religions. Fundamentalism in both science and religion reverse our progress.

As for those who wish to impose their will on us, well, the vast majority of them belong in the Third Party.

Sad... but true.

But then we do have the Few. They showed us that what we perceive with our primitive senses is but an illusion. They will also show us that we are the creators of our reality, and thus we can make it anything we want. Well, almost. Providing we don't bread any of the Universal Laws. It would help enormously if we knew what they are, it would eliminate the evolutionary method of trial and error.

And in this New Age of Aquarius, those Few will show us that Astral travel, dream control, bilocation, telepathy, metaphysical healing, even walking through walls will become perfectly normal modes of behaviour.

After all, we weren't called gods for nothing.

~~~~~

Finally, I can but hope that Albert Einstein, my hero and inspiration, would have accepted this humble submission of the *"Thoughts of God"*. After all, his theories made my reasoning possible, and for that, I shall forever remain grateful to him.

I hope that you, too, will accept them in the spirit in which they are offered. Day after tomorrow, we all might have fresh thoughts...

Jain Dharma, a word derived from the Sanskrit word jina, meaning 'victor', appear to have had the right idea.

We start in Eden, in Paradise. We now know that receiving 'skins' symbolizes our first step towards materiality. The first, erroneous, step of recognizing the phenomenal world as real.

The rest is history.

Luckily for us, evolution proceeds in cycles. When we reach a point of no return, we shall begin, once again, in Paradise. This time, hopefully, at a slightly higher rate of vibrations, i.e. at a higher stage of evolution, which will allow us, once again, to increase and enhance the Phenomenal Universe.

There is no hurry. After all, we are immortal.

And by the time we merge, again, with the Omnipresent Creative Energy of Consciousness, we shall guide new species, new diversities, onto the path of eternal enfoldment. Immortality and eternity are synonymous. We are fragment of each.

~~~~~~~~~~~

CONCLUSIONS

I may have mentioned various aspects of these thoughts before. Please, bear with me.

There are only two aspects to our reality. The **Potential** and the **Manifested**. *The Potential is the infinite, omnipresent, energy, vibrating at infinite frequency of the Creative Consciousness.* The Manifested is the Phenomenal Universe which is perceptible to our (as yet primitive) senses, which, in turn, is in constant metamorphosis, resulting from the Creative Consciousness's search for perfection extant in the Potential.

This search consists of metamorphosing the infinite frequency of vibration of the Original Potential Energy to lower frequencies, and thus creating diversity of expression extant in its potential form, i.e.: in the *Original Energy of the Omnipresent Consciousness.* This metamorphosis is a progressive process, most probably starting with the energy extant in the Omnipresent Mind (which appears to be a trait inherent or intrinsic to the Energy of the Creative Consciousness), and responds to the dictates of the Creative impulse, or nature of the Original Energy.

This appears to produce energies of light and sound, which in turn reduce the frequencies of vibration further until they become perceptible to our senses as our Phenomenal Universe.

There are many forms of light energy, the kinetic

forms being visible to human eye, and can be measured in angstrom and nanometers, hertz and electron volts (eV). Light, in turns, effect other forms of energy in the eternal process of metamorphosis.

There is one other means of adding diversity to the Phenomenal Universe. The creative impulse of Creative Consciousness has evolved a means which can generate its own creative energies. Such means is the human brain which can generate energies of creative thoughts. Those, in turn, contribute to producing new frequencies which are beyond the scope of the Omnipresent Energy. The reason is that the Energy of Omnipresent Consciousness can only produce perfect forms, hence limiting Its ability to produce added diversity. The human brain can generate energies which, though imperfect, they might be amenable to improvement and thus add to the diversity. Those energies that are not suitable, are, in time, accelerated to original frequencies in the hearts of Black Holes. Once accelerated, they are returned to the omnipresent Potential base from which all energies are emitted.

This thesis explains not only the continuous creative process but the expansion of the Phenomenal Universe. What we must accept that this process takes place in the eternal present.

In addition, we must accept that every single drop in the ocean bears the characteristics of the whole ocean. Hence, through the presence of the Consciousness of Higher Self in every single one of us, we each reflect the totality of the Phenomenal Universe with the state of our Consciousness. In this sense we, within the omnipresence of our Consciousness, are the whole universe. Not in the phenomenal but in the Potential sense. As such, to quote ancient prophets, we are gods. The 'godhood' within us is defined by absolute unification of our Higher Self with the Ego consciousness. This union allows us to perform "miracles" by manipulating the frequencies of vibrations of energies of the Phenomenal Universe.

This maxim has been asserted by Yeshûa (later known as Jesus) in the saying "I and my Father are one." As we shall be when we achieve this union of consciousness. After all, we now know that ALL IS ENERGY, and the original energy is the Omnipresent Energy of the Creative Consciousness vibrating at infinite frequency. As such it exists beyond the limitations of time or space.

Good luck!

***

APPENDIX
A Few Items that might Accelerate Change.

Unabated greenhouse gas emissions might cripple oceans phytoplankton's ability to produce oxygen.

Unprecedented costal erosion, already evident in Australia.

Swarms of locust might devour the world's crops. It happened in the distant past. Will it repeat itself?

Speed of metabolic evolution of other (perhaps anaerobic) species.

Wanton destruction caused by world sinking into a state of anarchy.

University of British Columbia astronomy student Michelle Kunimoto has discovered 17 new planets, including a potentially habitable, Earth-sized world, by combing through data gathered by NASA's Kepler mission. Are we on the move?

The mysterious planet 9, might prove to be a primordial grapefruit-sized black hole with a mass of five to ten times that of the Earth...
(www.sciencemag.org)

Other astrophysicists speculate that there may be hundreds of minor planets found beyond Neptune in our Solar System. We can but hope that all their orbits are stable, and not smash into us as they did in the past.

Aren't we lucky that we are immortal? And if you want to make sure, read my *KEY TO IMMORTALITY*. It may relax you for a while. Or... forever? Good luck.

NASA's asteroid hunters have identified yet another five close flybys due this week but, even more worryingly, they have also identified one space rock, which will soon pass between Earth and the Moon.

Enjoy every day. It might be your last! Ha, ha! Aren't you glad that you're immortal?

~~~~~~~~

A Word about the Author

Stanisław Kapuściński (aka **Stan I.S. Law**), architect, sculptor and prolific writer, was educated in Poland and England. Since 1965 he has resided in Canada. His special interests cover a broad spectrum of arts, sciences and philosophy. His fiction and non-fiction attest to his particular passion for the scope and the development of Human Potential. He has authored more than forty books, twenty of them novels.

Under his real name, he published non-fiction books sharing his vision of reality. He also composed two collections of poems in his original native tongue in which he satirizes his view of the world while paying homage to Bozena Happach's sculptures.

~~~~~

By the same author

Non-fiction

VISUALIZATION—Creating your own Universe
KEY TO IMMORTALITY
[Commentary on the Gospel of Thomas]
BEYOND RELIGION I
BEYOND RELIGION II
BEYOND RELIGION III
[Each volume contains 52 Essays on Perception of Reality]
DICTIONARY OF BIBLICAL SYMBOLISM
VICIOUS CIRCLE (Volumes 1 to 6)
[In search of Secular Ethics]
DELUSIONS—Pragmatic Realism
CONCLUSIONS—Pragmatic Reality
PSALM 23 — Exegesis
ISAIAH —The Birth of Higher Consciousness
THE LORD'S PRAYER
SELF EGO VIRUS
DECALOGUE

~~~~~~~

Fiction by Stan I.S. Law
(aka Stanisław Kapuściński)
Novels

WALL—Love, Sex & Immortality [Aquarius Trilogy Book I]
PLUTO EFFECT [Aquarius Trilogy Book II]
OLYMPUS — Of Gods and Men [Aquarius Trilogy Book III]
MARVIN CLARK—In Search of Freedom
GIFT OF GAMMAN
ENIGMA OF THE SECOND COMING
ONE JUST MAN [Winston Trilogy Book I]
ELOHIM—Masters & Minions [Winston Trilogy Book II]
WINSTON'S KINGDOM [Winston Trilogy Book III]
THE AVATAR SYNDROME [Avatar Trilogy Book I]
HEADLESS WORLD [Avatar Trilogy Book II]
AWAKENING [Avatar Trilogy Book III]
THE PRINCESS
ALEC [Alexander Trilogy Book I]
ALEXANDER [Alexander Trilogy Book II]
SACHA—The Way Back [Alexander Trilogy Book III]
YESHUA—Personal Memoir of the Missing Years of Jesus
THE GATE—Things my Mother told Me
NOW—Being and Becoming
ALEXANDER TRILOGY
AVATAR TRILOGY
AQUARIUS TRILOGY
WINSTON TRILOGY

Anthologies of Short Stories

THE JEWEL
CATS and DOGS Series
SCI-FI 1
SCI-FI 2

Poetry in Polish

KILKA SŁÓW I TROCHĘ GLINY
WIĘCEJ SŁÓW I WIĘCEJ GLINY